SCIENCE ON THE EDGE

SPACE TRAVEL

WRITTEN BY
TONEY ALLMAN

BLACKBIRCH PRESS
An imprint of Thomson Gale, a part of The Thomson Corporation

THOMSON
✦
GALE
™

Detroit • New York • San Francisco • San Diego • New Haven, Conn. • Waterville, Maine • London • Munich

LIBRARY OF CONGRESS CATALOGING-IN-PUBLICATION DATA

Allman, Toney.
  Space travel / by Toney Allman.
    p. cm. — (Science on the edge)
  Includes bibliographical references and index.
  ISBN 1-4103-0532-5 (hardcover : alk. paper)
  1. Astronautics—Juvenile literature. 2. Interplanetary voyages—Juvenile literature. I. Title. II. Series.

  TL793.A4545 2005
  629.45—dc22
                                  2004020614

TABLE OF CONTENTS

INTO THE SPACE AGE

Although much of the solar system has been explored and mapped by unmanned space vehicles and robotic probes, human space travel is the exciting and entertaining adventure that captures the imagination of the world and pushes forward the drive to conquer space. Yet space travel endangers human lives. Of the 243 manned spaceflights that have taken place during the forty-three years of the

The Sun reflects off Earth as an astronaut walks in space.

Space travel is an exciting but dangerous adventure that captures the world's imagination.

Buzz Aldrin walks on the Moon. Space travelers play an important role in humanity's future in space.

space age, 4 percent have resulted in the deaths of the pioneering space crews. Many more space explorers have faced problems and emergencies that put their lives at risk. The story of human spaceflight is a story of courage, of surmounting difficulties, and of starting over again in the face of failure. It is also the story of tremendous successes, both technological and personal.

If humankind is to have a future in space, as many believe it must, then both the successes and the failures have to be used as learning experiences and for inspiration so that one day space can become humanity's true home. All the space travelers of yesterday and today are contributing to that future.

CHAPTER 1

REACH FOR THE MOON

Ever since humans first turned their telescopes to the heavens and discovered that the Moon and planets were real worlds, people have yearned to explore these alien places. For hundreds of years it was possible only to look and to wonder. In the twentieth century, however, humanity's dream of traveling in space and to other worlds started to come true.

Early astronomers study the stars. People have wanted to explore outer space since the discovery that the Moon and planets are real worlds.

No one knew what value space travel could have for humanity. No one knew what discoveries awaited. Some people wondered why the dangers and costs of space travel should be risked at all. But human beings have always been curious about the unknown, and many people believed unpredictable benefits would result from space exploration. Two nations, the United States and the Soviet Union, in a spirit of technological and political competition, believed the effort to be worthwhile and wanted to prove it could be done.

Workers prepare an American rocket for launch. The United States and the Soviet Union believed space exploration was worthwhile.

NASA launched monkeys into space to see if living things could survive space travel.

The United States set up NASA (the National Aeronautics and Space Administration) in 1958 to coordinate and research space exploration. The Soviet Union also began an ambitious rocket and space travel program. At first, only unmanned vehicles were launched as scientists checked out the reliability of their spacecraft and their ability to guide the vehicles into orbit, reentry, and landing, all from ground stations. Then, living things such as insects, dogs,

The Soviet Union sent these dogs into orbit in the 1960s to test the difficulties of spaceflight.

and monkeys were launched into space. No one was sure that living beings could tolerate weightlessness in space or survive the rough ride through Earth's blanket of atmosphere. Nonhuman creatures proved that it was possible to live through a rocket trip.

Human space travel actually began on April 12, 1961, when Yuri Gagarin, a Russian cosmonaut, became the first man to orbit Earth. Throughout the early 1960s, as astronauts and cosmonauts were launched in ever bigger rockets with ever heavier, roomier capsules, scientists and engineers learned by experience how to protect humans and accommodate their needs for survival in space. All the early orbital flights were aimed at learning how to open space exploration for human beings.

People in space need special life support systems to keep them alive. From about 3 miles (4.8km) above Earth's surface, no air exists for people to breathe. Humans are built to function under the pressure that Earth's atmosphere exerts on their bodies. No such pressure exists in space. People need pressurized space suits and pressurized capsule cabins in order to survive. The pressurized suits and capsules must have oxygen pumped into them so astronauts can breathe normally.

As the speed of the rocket increased during a launch, astronauts experienced the equivalent of increasing forces of gravity. During the fastest periods of flight through the atmosphere these g-forces

Humans must wear pressurized space suits to survive in space.

A fireball burns around a space capsule as it reenters Earth's atmosphere.

caused the astronauts to weigh six times more than they did on the ground. The same effect occurred as the capsule braked hard during reentry. Astronauts had to be able to tolerate these g-forces as they accelerated or decelerated at the beginning or end of a spaceflight. They also had to be protected from the 1300 degrees Fahrenheit (704.4 degrees Celsius) temperatures created by friction as the capsule sped through the atmosphere on its return. Heat shields for space capsules were developed. Couches kept astronauts lying down with their feet higher than their heads during acceleration and deceleration. In this position, the blood would not drain from their heads to their legs and cause them to black out as g-forces dragged on their bodies.

THE APOLLO PROGRAM

With protective vehicles and equipment, healthy humans would suffer no ill effects from the hardships of space travel. As a matter of fact, astronauts and cosmonauts enjoyed weightlessness and reveled in their unique views of Earth. The space age had begun, and in 1961, President John F. Kennedy gave NASA an ambitious goal—to land a man on the Moon before the end of the decade. To meet this deadline, NASA instituted the Apollo program, a series of spaceflights and experiments to prepare for an eventual lunar flight. They knew a flight to the Moon would involve technology on the very edge of human capability.

It started with the Saturn rocket, which stood 363 feet (110.64m) tall—the largest, most powerful rocket ever built. Saturn was made up of over a million parts, each of which had to work perfectly. The three-stage rocket was able to lift 6 million pounds (272.5MT) away from Earth's atmosphere. At the top of the Saturn rocket sat the life support system for the astronauts. This space

An Apollo spacecraft awaits launch. NASA's Apollo program included a series of spaceflights and experiments to prepare for a flight to the Moon.

vehicle was big enough to hold three people in a command module, a lunar lander, and all the oxygen, water, food, fuel, and equipment needed to survive a 250,000-mile (402,336km) trip through space to the Moon.

Ten Apollo missions tested every component of the planned Moon mission so that scientists, designers, engineers, medical doctors, and astronauts could be sure that the flight would succeed. Yet tragedy struck the mission of *Apollo 1*. As three astronauts sat locked in their capsule atop the Saturn rocket at the launchpad,

An oxygen fire sparked by a frayed electrical wire destroyed the *Apollo 1* capsule. Three astronauts died when fire swept the capsule's interior (inset).

Astronauts Ed White (left), Gus Grissom (center), and Ron Chaffee (right) lost their lives in the *Apollo I* fire.

testing the oxygen system, a frayed electrical wire sparked beneath one of the seats. The capsule had been pressurized with pure oxygen, and that oxygen caused a raging fire. Unable to open the capsule's hatch, Gus Grissom, Ron Chaffee, and Ed White died before their mission ever left Earth.

The disaster horrified NASA and people across the United States. NASA shut down its Apollo program temporarily, studied all its systems, and used the tragedy to learn what went wrong and correct the faulty technology that led to the fire. Engineers designed a new escape hatch for the capsule, so that in an emergency astronauts could escape within six seconds. They bundled the miles of electrical wires into insulating tubes so that no spark could escape into the capsule. They changed the atmospheric oxygen mix to reduce the fire hazard. Velcro, cloth, plastic materials, and

THE SOVIET SPACE PROGRAM

Cosmonaut Vladimir Komarov died in 1967 when a failed solar panel crippled his spacecraft.

The Soviet Union was in a race with the United States to be first on the Moon, but a series of rocket failures and explosions derailed Soviet efforts. The Soviet space program faced its share of human tragedies, too. In 1967, Soviet cosmonaut Vladimir Komarov was orbiting Earth in a Soyuz spacecraft when a solar panel on his ship failed to open. At that time, Soviet capsules depended on these solar "wings" to provide electrical power for all the ships' systems. Komarov soon found himself fighting a crippled, rolling capsule that could not fly or be automatically guided back to Earth. Komarov knew his chances of manually bringing the capsule into reentry were poor, but he courageously tried. First, while still in orbit, he spoke by radio to his wife for the last time. Then, he successfully guided the capsule into a speeding reentry. But the capsule continued to tumble out of control. The parachutes used to slow the capsule's descent tangled and wrapped around the capsule. Komarov crashed into the ground at 400 miles (643.7km) per hour.

In 1971, a successful month-long flight to an early Soviet space station ended in the deaths of three more cosmonauts. They were returning to Earth in their spacecraft when a valve failed without warning and allowed the entire atmosphere to stream out of the small ship. When the recovery team arrived at the site of a perfect landing, all three cosmonauts were found dead. It was the first and only fatal decompression in a spaceflight.

aluminum surfaces were fireproofed. When the Apollo missions resumed, thirteen hundred design changes had been made.

In subsequent missions, all Apollo systems were tested and improved as scientists learned more. Astronauts practiced living in weightlessness in Earth orbit for the eight days a Moon trip would take. Scientists carefully measured their bodies' reactions to be sure that they could tolerate such conditions. The astronauts practiced eating in space. They ate dried food, packed in pouches, that could be mixed with hot water and eaten with a spoon. They learned to go to the bathroom in plastic bags and hoses designed by engineers. They experimented with their ship's thrusters, making sure that they could maneuver their space vehicle into and out of Moon orbit. They learned to walk in space and control their heavy space suits.

HUMANS TO THE MOON

Finally, in 1969, *Apollo 11* was ready to launch a mission that would land on the Moon. It was the best and safest spaceship available, but it operated with primitive computers that had less memory than a calculator watch of today. Its radio communication with Earth was often interrupted. NASA's ground relay stations could not talk to the ship continuously. No rescue in space was possible either. If any of the millions of parts on the spaceship malfunctioned, the astronauts would have to fix it themselves, do without it, or be lost. But the three astronauts who flew to the Moon were not completely on their own. NASA mission control had thousands of scientists and specialists on the ground who communicated with the astronauts, tracked the ship and its systems from Earth, and did everything possible to keep the astronauts safe.

The astronauts were connected by electrodes to medical monitoring systems that told doctors on Earth how their hearts, digestive systems, blood pressures, and lungs were functioning during their voyage. The astronauts also carried television cameras

Buzz Aldrin left his footprint (inset) on the surface of the Moon during his July 20, 1969, lunar landing.

The *Apollo 13* astronauts used socks and duct tape to fix the spaceship's breathing systems.

so that all the people of Earth could share in their historic first steps on the Moon.

On July 20, 1969, Neil Armstrong became the first human being to step onto the Moon. He and his fellow astronaut, Buzz Aldrin, left a plaque on the Moon that expressed the wonder and joy of humanity's first experience on another world: "Here, men from the planet Earth first set foot on the Moon, July 1969 A.D. We came in peace for all mankind."[1]

Apollo missions 12, 14, 15, 16, and 17 returned to the Moon, collected more than 800 pounds (362.9kg) of Moon rocks, drove lunar rovers over distances of a few miles in minivoyages of discovery, and extended scientific knowledge about the practicality of a future lunar station. *Apollo 13* was meant to travel to the Moon but became a dramatic lesson in near disaster instead. A part in the space vehicle malfunctioned, caused an explosion, and crippled the ship. With the help of hundreds of mission specialists on the ground, astronauts Jim Lovell, Fred Haise, and Jack Swigart figured out how to return home in a ship with little oxygen, electric power, or temperature controls.

The marooned travelers learned to repair breathing systems with duct tape and socks. They developed ways to conserve water, to survive in freezing temperatures, and to guide a damaged spaceship through atmospheric reentry without computer help. *Apollo 13* became known as "the successful failure" because NASA succeeded in its first space rescue and learned how to cope with emergencies that threatened lives in space.

THE END FOR APOLLO

With the technology and knowledge gained from Apollo, NASA enthusiastically planned future missions to build space stations, design reusable space shuttles, and launch humans to Mars by the end of the century. It was not to be, however. In 1972, the United States government canceled NASA's plans and severely cut its budget. The Moon was never visited again.

One program remained to NASA, the development of a reusable space shuttle. In the Soviet Union, where Moon flight efforts were never successful, attention turned to the development of a space station and research into long-term space living. The exploration of new worlds was no longer a priority, but space travel would continue in new ways.

CHAPTER 2

MAINTAINING HUMAN PRESENCE IN SPACE

After Apollo, human space travel was confined to Earth orbit, about 100 to 300 miles (161.9 to 482.8km) above Earth. The United States concentrated on development of the Space Transportation System, or shuttle orbiter. The Soviet Union used its knowledge and experience to develop space stations and ultimately build the space station Mir. When the Soviet Union broke up, NASA and the Russian space program formed a partnership that led to an international effort to advance human space travel.

The Soviet Mir space station orbits Earth. The Russian space program and NASA began working together after the Soviet Union's breakup.

THE SPACE SHUTTLE

The space shuttle *Challenger* explodes on January 28, 1986, just minutes after launch.

The American space shuttle made its first orbital flight in 1981. The shuttle was a large spacecraft, able to provide a crew of seven with living, sleeping, eating, and working quarters. Scientists and mission specialists, as well as astronauts, could ride in the shuttle because it was so safe and comfortable. Shuttle flights went so smoothly that they seemed routine. President Ronald Reagan even joked with one shuttle crew that he would make a flight himself some day.

Confidence in the safety of shuttle orbiters was severely shaken, however, on January 28, 1986, when the shuttle *Challenger* blew up minutes after launch. All seven astronauts aboard were killed. NASA shut down the shuttle program as it investigated the cause of the disaster and made changes in the shuttle design. A grieving United States realized that space travel would always be full of risks.

When shuttle flights resumed, three years after the *Challenger* disaster, they were as safe as NASA could make them, but the shuttles really had no place to go. In 1993, President Bill Clinton decided that linking with the Russians was the answer.

MIR SPACE STATION

The Russians and NASA modified Mir so that space shuttles could dock with it.

Russia had maintained its space station Mir in Earth orbit for ten years. Mir was made up of modules linked together by narrow crawlways through hatches. It also had a Soyuz spacecraft in dock as an emergency escape vehicle. Russian cosmonauts had lived aboard Mir for a year at a time. Unmanned cargo ships docked regularly with Mir to resupply the station. When NASA and the Russians became partners, they reconfigured the shuttles and Mir so that shuttles could also dock at the station. American astronauts joined Russian cosmonauts for long-term missions. Shuttles helped supply Mir with equipment, scientific devices, and fresh food.

SURVIVING ON MIR

Mir was an aging, dilapidated station where systems often broke down. Near disasters on Mir gave American and Russian space dwellers hands-on experience in how to cope with emergencies far from any help on Earth. One day, for example, cosmonaut Gennady Strekalov scraped his arm when he reached behind a panel. By the next day, the arm was blue, swollen, and infected from wrist to shoulder. Doctors on Earth could give advice, but not help. Crew members with a medical kit had to take over. After several anxious days and many pills, Strekalov's arm slowly healed.

A more serious emergency aboard Mir involved fire. Six crewmen were aboard Mir in 1997, three newly arrived to take over the station and three who had lived there for several months. Most

A cosmonaut works aboard the aging Mir. Near disasters aboard the space station provided valuable experience in coping with emergencies in space.

SWIMMING THROUGH WEIGHTLESSNESS

Floating in weightlessness is a lot of fun, but it can mean learning new skills. On Mir, for example, new crew members moved from one end of a module to the other by kicking off from a wall and then diving through the air with their arms stretched protectively in front of them. Experienced cosmonauts just dove headfirst with arms down by their sides. Once in a while, though, a newcomer would bump into an expert "swimmer" and make him or her bang an unprotected head into a wall. Even in weightlessness, a bump on the head hurts.

Newcomers to space may also forget that they cannot move in weightlessness without pushing away

An astronaut prepares for
weightless travel through Mir.

Astronauts and cosmonauts share
a weightless meal in space.

from something. On the International Space Station
(ISS) some astronauts would forget to push off hard
enough to make it to another solid object. Then the
unlucky astronaut would find himself or herself stuck in
midmodule with no way to get anywhere. When that
happened, the embarrassed astronaut would have to
call for someone else to come give a helpful push. A
few days in space will teach all space crews to
navigate well, but they do have to learn quickly that
Earth walking is very different from space station
swimming.

were gathered in the base module, when Sasha Lazutkin went through the hatch into the next module to perform a routine duty. He had to drop a new oxygen canister into the supplemental system that provided extra air while the other men were living on the station. Lazutkin dropped the canister into place, turned the dial to activate it, and watched in shock as a foot-long flame (0.30m) shot from the canister.

Mir commander Valery Korzun dove through the hatch to the rescue. His fire extinguisher, switched to foam setting, did no good. Supported by the oxygen, the fire grew 2 feet (0.61m) long, belched thick, black smoke, and blew bits of glowing foam out into the air. Korzun ordered the crew into oxygen masks and called for more fire extinguishers. In the cramped crawlway, Korzun fought the fire with extinguishers passed to him by his crewmates. The smoke billowed into the base module and turned everything dark as Korzun switched his fire extinguisher to water and aimed for the glow in the blackness. A third extinguisher was passed to him. The white glow gradually grew smaller, and the fire finally died.

American astronaut Jerry Linenger was a doctor and checked the crew for breathing problems from the black smoke that hung everywhere. Linenger found everyone in good health, but he gave them all surgical masks to wear until the atmosphere could be cleared. Automatic oxygen scrubbers worked to clean the smoke away. The soot left on every surface had to be cleaned away by hand. When their jobs were done, the men were exhausted, but they had saved themselves and their station from the worst fire ever to occur in space.

DECOMPRESSION!

Just a few months later, two of the men who experienced that fire, Sasha Lazutkin and Vasily Tsibliyev, faced an even worse emergency. By that time, Tsibliyev was commander of Mir, and astronaut Michael Foale had replaced Linenger as the American crew

Failed braking controls caused an unmanned cargo ship to crash into Mir and damage a solar panel.

member. Tsibliyev was attempting to dock an unmanned cargo ship with Mir when the braking controls failed. The ship flew in too fast and crashed into Mir. It smashed a solar panel on Mir's hull that provided power to the station. Worse, it punctured a quarter-size hole in the hull of one of Mir's modules. "Oh, hell!" yelled Tsibliyev. "We have decompression!"[2] Mir's hull had been breached, and its atmosphere was streaming out into space. The men had only minutes to decide whether to evacuate the station or try to find and seal the breach.

Foale and Lazutkin rushed to the module where the decompression had taken place. They could hear the air hissing out, but in the blackness of the power failure, they could not find the hole. Lazutkin decided to try to seal off the module from the rest of the station by closing the hatch. Foale frantically tried to help Lazutkin, while Tsibliyev communicated the emergency to Russian mission control and opened the emergency oxygen tanks on the station. The extra oxygen would give the men more minutes of life as they fought to stop the leak.

Lazutkin and Foale could not close the hatch. The station's atmosphere streamed through the hatchway and created suction so strong that the two men could not pull shut the hatch door against the flow of escaping air. Then Lazutkin remembered the hatch cover that hung on the wall. It looked like a garbage can lid and was used as an extra seal for the hatch door. Quickly he cut it from the straps where it hung, and he and Foale carried it to the hatch opening. The stream of escaping air helped them then. The cover was sucked tightly into place, sealing off the leaking module from the rest of the station.

The station was saved, and the oxygen from Tsibliyev's emergency tanks was raising the air pressure, but Mir was still in trouble. Half the electric power was gone because of the damaged solar panel. The station was spinning slowly in space so that other solar arrays were receiving no power from the Sun. The temperature was dropping, and batteries were dying. The crew floated in blackness as the lighting aboard Mir failed. Neither Mir nor its crew could survive long without the systems that functioned by electricity.

With advice from mission control, the men gradually brought their crippled home back to life. They figured out how to stop the station's roll, aimed their solar panels at the Sun, recharged their batteries, and fixed computer systems. As life got back to normal, they even found time for entertainment. Foale showed the Russians the movie *Apollo 13*, about the long-ago crisis on the failed trip to the Moon. It became Tsibliyev's favorite movie.

INTERNATIONAL SPACE STATION

Through the many crises aboard Mir, Russians and Americans learned that space travelers could survive and solve more problems in space than anyone thought. Both countries discovered that they could learn from each other and work together. The shuttle-Mir program led to an agreement to build a better, safer station—the International Space Station (ISS). It is a cooperative effort by NASA, the Russian space program, the European Space Agency, Canada, and Japan.

The International Space Station has been orbiting Earth since the first module was launched by Russia in 1998. Humans have permanently occupied the station since 2000. It is made up of four modules and has giant solar panels that collect solar energy to power the station's systems. Both shuttles and Soyuz vessels ferried mission specialists and cargo to and from the station.

The ISS is more comfortable, roomy, and practical for human living and working than either Mir or a shuttle. It has real toilets, a

An astronaut works in space on the International Space Station. Building the space station is a collaborative effort of sixteen nations.

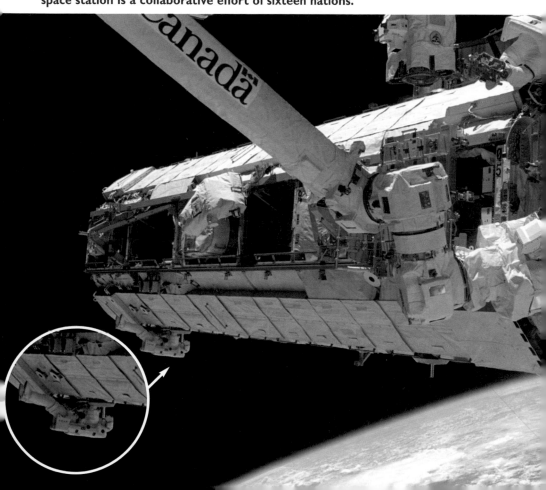

The crew members of the space shuttle *Columbia* lost their lives on February 1, 2003, when the craft exploded in Earth's atmosphere.

kitchen, sleeping hammocks, exercise equipment, and laboratories for scientific work. Station crew members became very skilled at coping with repairs in space, docking with cargo ships, taking space walks to maintain the station, and just living in space for long stretches of time. Life in space began to feel ordinary and safe until a tragedy occurred.

DEATH AND DETERMINATION

On February 1, 2003, the shuttle *Columbia* was returning home from an ISS mission when it exploded in the atmosphere, killing all seven astronauts aboard. NASA immediately shut down the shuttle program while it investigated the cause of the tragedy and redesigned the shuttle program to guard against future accidents. The ISS could no longer be supplied by shuttle flights.

The *Columbia* disaster could have severely affected ISS operations, but Russia took over. With Soyuz vessels, the Russians have kept the space station supplied and ferried crew members back and forth. Shuttle flights are scheduled to resume in 2005, but until that time, international dedication and determination are keeping Earth's space efforts alive. The next step in space exploration is a return to deep space missions.

CHAPTER 3

DESTINATION: DEEP SPACE

Experience has taught humanity that space travel is risky, but these dangers have not discouraged people with the urge to explore new frontiers. In 2004, President George W. Bush gave the international space program and NASA new life when he proposed a far-reaching plan to return to deep space missions. The plan is to visit the Moon between 2015 and 2020, and send a human mission to Mars by 2030.

RETURN TO THE MOON

NASA's return to the Moon will be different from the Apollo missions. The modern Moon missions will engineer and design technologies that make it possible for people to live on the Moon for extended periods of time. The Moon will be NASA's practice field. It is in Earth's backyard, and everything needed for a trip to Mars can be developed and tested there, close to the safety of Earth. A lunar base will be established, human habitats will be invented, and Moon resources will be used.

One idea for astronaut homes on the Moon is called a "Habot." A Habot would be a module, like space station modules, but with six legs, wheels, and robotic controls. Several Habots could be flown to the Moon and landed at different sites. Then the robot modules would walk away to a preselected base. The Habots could meet at this base, link to form a large habitat structure, and wait for astronauts to arrive. Astronauts would arrive at the Moon base to find a convenient home ready and waiting for them. The Habots will be mobile, too. Astronauts could undock a module and take off across the lunar surface on voyages of discovery or to mine lunar

A model shows how robotic modules might be used to establish a base on the Moon.

resources. Several modules could travel linked together in a lunar wagon train.

The Habot crew will have to be protected from radiation, both from the Sun and from outside the solar system, while they are living in the module or working on the lunar surface. Earth's magnetic field protects humans from this deadly radiation, even in Earth orbit. On the Moon, no such protection exists. People in space for long periods of time will need special radiation shields. Scientists at NASA are already working on materials for space suits and Habots that will keep astronauts safe from cosmic radiation.

In protective space suits, astronauts will walk the lunar surface and, with the help of robots, mine the Moon for water. Unmanned missions have shown that water is frozen into the Moon's surface. Astronauts will use the mined water not only for drinking, but also for making air to breathe and fuel for rocket trips away from the Moon.

For NASA, the experience gained at a lunar base would provide the knowledge and ability to launch deep space missions to Mars and beyond. It would be the first step in conquering the solar system, but NASA is not the only group interested in the Moon. Private organizations and societies are planning Moon and space expeditions, not just for well-trained astronauts, but to open up space travel for everyone.

SPACE TOURISM

In 1995, the Ansari X Prize was established by a group of private citizens who dreamt of flying into space. Ten million dollars was offered to the first person or business that could launch a spacecraft of three people, or their weight equivalent, 62 miles (100km) into

SpaceShipOne **makes a test flight over California in preparation for the Ansari X Prize competition.**

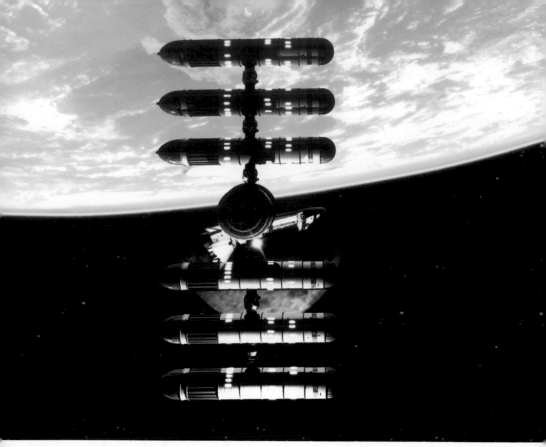

Earth-orbiting space hotels like the one in this computer-generated illustration may one day attract tourists.

space, and then repeat the flight with the same vehicle within two weeks. Two dozen teams around the world competed for the prize. On October 4, 2004, the vehicle *SpaceShipOne* won the competition when it successfully completed its second flight, with a pilot and two sacks of mementos that weighed as much as two passengers. The designer of *SpaceShipOne*, Burt Rutan, already is planning the design of a second, eight-passenger vehicle that will open space travel to tourists. Rutan believes that regular tourist space flights are less than fifteen years away. For about $30,000, tourists will be able to fly in space and take snapshots of Earth. Next, he says, hotels will be built in Earth orbit. People will be able to play games such as racquetball in weightlessness or invent their own flying games. When that happens, lunar tourism will not be long in coming. A private organization, The Moon Society, is working and planning for that goal.

The Moon Society developed the Artemis Project, a business venture to build a permanent lunar base with a Moon hotel and provide commercial flights for tourists to the Moon. The Artemis Project says to everyone, "*You* can come, too!"[3] The Artemis Project will be financed by companies in the business of entertaining people and profiting from tourism. Moon flight will no longer belong only to the government. The project already has plans in place for the Luna City Hotel. Tourists will fly to the Moon in a commercial spaceship, ride pressurized buses to the towering hotel, and stay in luxurious rooms with magnificent views of Earth and space. They will take walking tours in their space suits to collect Moon rocks or see the spot where Neil Armstrong first stepped on

The Moon Society's Artemis Project hopes to establish a Moon hotel with Earth views.

lunar soil. The Artemis Project believes such a vacation will be possible in about twenty years at a cost of around $100,000 per person. Perhaps, at the same time that tourists flock to the Moon hotel, NASA will be ready to launch its first human mission to Mars.

A HUMAN TRIP TO MARS

No matter how much experience people have with living on the Moon, a trip to Mars will still be difficult and dangerous. On the Moon, people are only two or three days away from help, advice, or rescue from Earth. A trip to Mars would take three years before the crew would again see home. Expert space explorers, not tourists, will make the Mars voyage. The crew will have to be independent

An injured space explorer receives first aid in this illustration. The distance from Mars to Earth adds to the danger of Mars exploration.

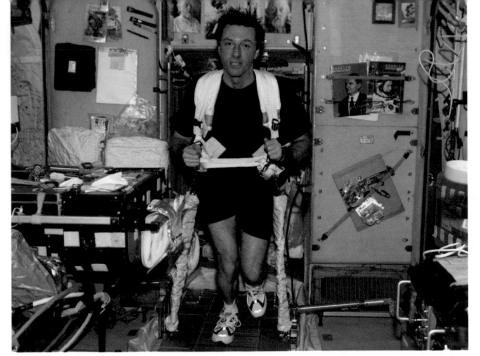

An astronaut aboard the International Space Station exercises on a treadmill to fight the physical weakness caused by prolonged weightlessness.

of Earth resources for a long, long time. Mars is 122 million miles (196.3 million km) away. Radio signals take eleven minutes to travel between Earth and Mars. Space emergencies will have to be handled without help from mission ground controls. Nevertheless, NASA astronauts and space explorers around the world yearn to make the trip.

Much has been learned from Mir and the International Space Station about adapting to long space missions. A crew of six on a Mars voyage would use that knowledge to stay healthy and comfortable during the long trip. Over the years, NASA has learned that about half the people who travel in weightlessness develop Space Adaptation Syndrome. People with this problem suffer nausea and vomiting when their digestive systems shut down in space conditions. Medical researchers are studying ways to predict which people might have this problem and what medicines might reverse it.

Crew members in space must also fight the physical weakness that prolonged weightlessness causes. Treadmills and other exercise

INVENTIONS FROM THE SPACE PROGRAM

While NASA works to advance human space travel, it develops many new technologies and devices that eventually become welcome and useful tools on Earth. Cordless power tools, for example, were invented by Black and Decker when NASA's Apollo program asked the company to develop a tool the astronauts could use to drill into the Moon's surface. Smoke detectors are another invention that started with NASA. Because of the dangers of fire in space, NASA asked Honeywell Inc. to develop a smoke and fire detector to protect astronauts sleeping in space. Smoke detectors are now used in almost all American homes, but before human space travel, no one had ever thought of them.

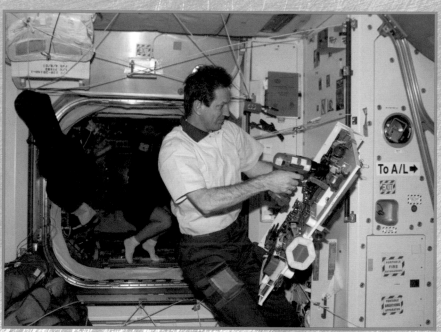

A cosmonaut uses a cordless drill during his work at the International Space Station.

Miniature transmitters that can actually be swallowed or inserted under the skin are a NASA invention, too. These transmitters are only as big as a pill, and astronauts on the ISS use them so that doctors on the ground can keep track of the astronauts' blood pressure and temperature. Astronauts prefer the pills to the bothersome old-fashioned wires and electrodes they used to have to wear. Doctors in American hospitals are adapting this technology to help people on Earth. The transmitters can be implanted in a mother's womb to keep track of how her baby is developing during pregnancy. If the transmitter detects trouble, doctors can intervene right away. Other medical scientists are experimenting with using these transmitters to monitor people with very dangerous jobs, such as firefighters and soldiers. The transmitters would send data to medical personnel who would be instantly alerted if a soldier or firefighter was in physical trouble. Some day, transmitters such as these may save people all over the world from heart attacks or other health emergencies. Space technology can benefit not just astronauts, but all the people on Earth.

A Mars explorer examines a rock in this illustration. Exploration of Mars may reveal forms of life on the planet.

equipment will be used to keep hearts, muscles, and bones from deteriorating during the months the astronauts are aboard the spaceship. Their psychological well-being will be considered, too. They will have gardens to tend, not only for fresh food, but also to help them relax. They will have music, reading material, games, and movies to combat boredom. No one knows, however, how lonely and isolated the crew may feel when Earth has receded to a small blue speck in the vastness of space. The trip to Mars will demand a lot of courage.

Once the Mars ship finally arrives and lands on that alien planet, the astronauts will use the technology developed on the Moon to make a livable environment. Perhaps they will live in Habots. Perhaps they will have an inflatable home, somewhat like an enclosed tent. They might use rovers to explore the planet in their space suits. They will seek out the frozen water on Mars and use it for drinking, to make oxygen for breathing, and to produce fuel for their spaceship when they are ready to return to Earth.

The Mars crew may even discover primitive life on the red planet. If they do, it will be only bacteria or fungi that have survived Mars's harsh environmental conditions. Discovering any form of life, however, would answer one of Earth's greatest questions. It would tell humanity if it is alone or if life is possible on other worlds, if life might be common or if it is incredibly rare. Life discovered on Mars would increase the chance of humans finding intelligent life somewhere in the galaxy.

HUMANITY'S FUTURE

By the time humans have landed on Mars, Earth will have identified which of the stars nearest to Earth have planets orbiting them. It may even be possible to tell if any of the planets are Earth-like. Then, NASA's challenge will be to somehow leave the solar system and travel to even farther frontiers. Before that happens, Saturn's

Terraforming could someday transform Mars into a human-friendly place.

moons may be visited and permanent space colonies, somewhat like huge space stations, may orbit the Sun. The Moon and Mars may hold colonies of Earth people who are starting new homelands just as Pilgrims did in America long ago.

Mars may even be "terraformed" into a planet where human beings can walk unprotected beneath its red sky. The idea that a whole planet's climate can be transformed into a human-friendly one used to be science fiction. Today, however, scientists consider terraforming a real possibility. Terraforming Mars would mean heating up the thin, dry, cold atmosphere until gases are trapped and temperatures rise. This greenhouse effect could be accomplished, for example, by using huge mirrors at the Martian poles to reflect the Sun's heat onto the frozen carbon dioxide on the surface. Over a period of many years, the climate of Mars could be altered until it was another Earth where green plants could grow and people could live.

Terraforming Mars and establishing artificial space colonies are far in the future, but they represent a future that will be achieved because of the space exploration that continues today. The space age is really just beginning. From the first orbital flight to the International Space Station, Earth's human space travelers have been pioneering the way to colonizing the solar system and eventually the stars. Because of them and the dangers they have overcome, Earth's children of today may be the Lunarites and Martians of tomorrow.

GLOSSARY

air pressure The amount of pressure Earth's atmosphere exerts on an object or person.

cosmic radiation High-energy particles from outer space that easily penetrate and pass through bodies and can disrupt normal functions, cause cancer, or be fatal if exposure is prolonged.

decompression The sudden loss of atmospheric pressure and the breathable air in a spacecraft, usually due to a puncture in the ship.

g-forces A measure of increased gravity-like forces during spacecraft acceleration and deceleration. As g-forces multiply, body weight effects multiply.

Habot A mobile robotic habitat for use by lunar landing crews.

magnetic field The effect generated by Earth's core which makes the planet a giant magnet, with lines of magnetism running from the North Pole to the South Pole.

orbit To make a complete revolution around a celestial body, such as Earth.

reentry The return of a spacecraft into Earth's atmosphere.

terraform To modify a planet or moon so that it has a changed climate, breathable atmosphere, and a habitable environment. Terraforming literally means Earth-shaping.

NOTES

Chapter 1: Reach for the Moon
1. Quoted in David West Reynolds, *Apollo: The Epic Journey to the Moon*. New York: Tehabi, 2002, p. 147.

Chapter 2: Maintaining Human Presence in Space
2. Quoted in Bryan Burrough, *Dragonfly: NASA and the Crisis Aboard Mir*. New York: HarperCollins, 1998, pp. 372–373.

Chapter 3: Destination: Deep Space
3. Artemis Project, "Brief Overview of the Artemis Project," www.asi.org/adb/01/brief-overview.html.

FOR FURTHER INFORMATION

Books

Barbara Bondar with Roberta Bondar, *On the Shuttle: Eight Days in Space*. Toronto, Ontario: Owl Greey de Pencier, 1993.

Stuart A. Kallen, *Apollo Moonwalkers*. Edina, MN: ABDO, 1996.

Don Nardo, *The Moon*. San Diego: KidHaven, 2002.

Peggy J. Parks, *Exploring Mars*. San Diego: Lucent, 2004.

Web Sites

About Space and Astronomy for Kids (http://space.about.com/od/educationastronomyspace/a/kidsastronomy.htm). Space and astronomy news for kids is available for many different topics. Different links describe the solar system, human space travel, and even the search for intelligent extraterrestrial life.

The Artemis Project (www.asi.org). The tour guides are a joke, but by clicking the different links you can learn the society's plan for your space trip to the Moon and your stay at the Lunar City Hotel. Take a virtual tour of the planned Moon base.

First Science, Part 2 of 4—Moon Landing (www.firstscience.com/site/video/part2.asp). Watch a video clip of actual Apollo Moon landings. Hear Neil Armstrong utter the first words ever spoken on the Moon.

Mars Tour (www.marsquestonline.org/mer). Humans have not yet visited Mars, but two Mars rovers named *Spirit* and *Opportunity* are already there and taking pictures of the red planet. This site offers a virtual photographic tour of where they have been and what they have discovered.

NASA for Students, Grades 5–8 (www.nasa.gov/audience/forstudents/5-8/features/index.html). Explore the official NASA Web site and learn about current astronauts, space missions, and space discoveries. Get up-to-the-minute NASA news.

INDEX